GIZMO

Goes to Germany

Copyright © 2025 Heidi Heisel

All rights reserved. No part of this publication may be reproduced, distributed or transmitted in any form or by any means, including photocopying, recording, or other electronic or mechanical methods, without the prior written permission of the author.

eBook Designed by

DEDICATION

This book is dedicated to HARIBO for inventing Gummy Bears in 1922.

Gizmo is the hero.
He's there to save the day.
Buzz Buzz Beep Biz...
The alarm makes it all go away.

Gizmo hit the snooze again,
and then again once more.
It was an everyday routine,
before his paws hit the floor.

Gizmo opened his eyes.
Oh no, not again.
He was going to be late for class,
and Fritz never waits to begin.

Fritz is the trainer,
at Service Dog School.
He's over the top strict,
and never breaks the rules.

Gizmo tip-toed in,
and slunk into his seat.
Fritz said loudly,
"Anything you vant me to repeat?"

Fritz is a German Shepard,
a breed known for being tough.
He was annoyed with Gizmo,
and he had had enough!

Fritz asked Gizmo,
to stay behind after class.
Gizmo was not too thrilled either,
why couldn't Fritz just relax?

"Gizmo you have a problem.
You're not going to graduate.
Your skills are excellent,
but you're constantly late."

"Service Dogs are helpers.
We are here to serve.
You're not disciplined enough,
from what I've observed."

"It's ok to be average,
lots of breeds are.
But to go from good to great,
you have to work hard."

Gizmo dropped his book bag,
no, this couldn't be.
He begged Fritz for another chance,
to prove himself worthy.

Fritz challenged Gizmo.
"Only if you come with me.
I have one make up class,
in my home country of Germany."

"Willkommen in Deutschland",
read the sign above.
Fritz spent the entire flight,
telling Gizmo about the land that he loves.

"Germany has more Castles than McDonalds,
between twenty and twenty-five thousand.
They invent all the best things like,
helicopters, computers, tv, bikes, and aspirin."

"The automobile, printing press and microscope,
are a few more German inventions.
Along with x-rays, airbags, the accordion,
and too many more to mention."

Fritz was still talking,
as they jumped on a train.
Gizmo thinks he even saw him smile,
as he waved Auf Wiedersehen.

Their first stop was Cologne,
a two thousand year old city on the Rhine.
Fritz wanted to show Gizmo the Gothic Cathedral,
a lesson in precision, discipline and time.

It took over six centuries,
to complete the build.
That's six hundred years,
of determination and will.

Gizmo was in awe,
he's never seen anything so grand.
The Cathedral is a masterpiece,
of Gothic perfection.

Fritz then took Gizmo,
to smell the world's first cologne.
Named Forty-Seven Eleven,
after the street it was created on.

Gizmo inhaled deeply,
and instantly closed his eyes.
He felt like he was floating in a meadow,
smelling rainbows and butterflies.

"That was two hundred and twenty-five years ago,"
the cashier explained to Fritz.
"It's known as miracle water."
Gizmo continued to spritz.

Gizmo was enjoying his own aroma,
as the hotel desk clerk took a sniff.
"Du riechst gut!" he said,
and took a second whiff.

Fritz dropped off Gizmo,
at his hotel room door.
"Meet me in the lobby at eight.
Tomorrow's class starts with a tour."

Gizmo's phone and tablet,
were both going dead.
When his plug didn't fit into the wall,
he called the front desk.

"Yes, German outlets require special plugs.
I'm surprised you didn't know.
It's in all the paperwork,
I guess you didn't read it though."

Gizmo was panic stricken,
he didn't know what to do.
He couldn't admit he wasn't prepared,
when lack of discipline was his whole issue.

He called the desk again and asked for
a seven a.m. wake up call,
and a book to help him fall asleep.
There would be no scrolling after all.

Cinderella, Red Riding Hood and Snow White,
all by the Brothers Grimm.
The original fairy tales,
translated as originally written.

Some light reading was perfect,
the day was already long.
He began to read and drift off to sleep,
but that's when things went wrong.

One evil stepsister lost her big toe,
and the other lost her heel.
The glass slipper never fit,
and their eyes became a pigeon's meal.

The wolf does eat grandma,
and Red Riding Hood too.
The Queen in Snow White,
is forced to dance in red hot iron shoes.

Gizmo was wide awake.
What kind of stories are these?
What happened to happily ever after?
And why is it half past three?

Gizmo is the hero.
He's here to save the day.
Ring Ring Ring Ring...
The big bad wolf takes grandma away.

He's back with the dwarfs.
There to save the day.
Ring Ring Ring Ring ...
The phone makes it all go away.

"Gizmo, wake up!
It's fifteen minutes to eight!
Fritz is on his way to the lobby!"
Gizmo sat up straight.

Oh no, not again.
There is no time to waste.
Gizmo threw on his clothes,
and gargled with straight toothpaste.

He ran down the hall,
then down the stairs.
He cooly walked into the lobby,
and the whole class just stared.

Gizmo looked at Fritz,
then up at the clock.
He was not late,
it was eight a.m. on the dot.

"Class meet Gizmo,
he's here for a make up exam.
Please excuse the pee pad,
stuck to the back of his pants."

The entire class giggled,
Gizmo couldn't help but laugh too.
He was a complete mess,
and he had on two different shoes.

Fritz looked at Gizmo,
and said, "You come sit with me.
Today is Feiertag,
a day meant for fun and discovery."

They took a bus to Bad Munstereifel,
a healing mineral spa city.
Protected by a medieval wall,
built in the thirteenth century.

Germany is a mix,
of the old and the new.
Traditional flowers on window sills,
and modern architecture too.

Fritz showed Gizmo,
the picturesque scenic view.
Then he pointed at a single brick in the wall.
"It all starts with you."

"One brick at a time,
every single day.
That's dedication and discipline,
the good old German way."

"The world doesn't reward effort,
It only rewards evidence.
It's that little extra every day,
that makes all the difference."

"You have great skills,
and you don't easily admit defeat.
But it's hard to see you as a Service Dog,
with the wrong shoes on your feet."

"It's the little things,
that make big things great.
Confidence starts when you can trust yourself,
not to be late."

"Hold yourself accountable,
no excuses, no blame.
Set clear goals,
tardiness is lame."

"Embrace hard work,
even when it's the pits.
Greatness is built on consistency,
long after everyone else quits."

This wall has protected the city,
for over eight hundred years.
Built by the Counts of Julich's,
German Engineers."

Fritz rounded up the class,
and everyone found a seat.
This time Gizmo sat next to Sophie,
a little girl so cute and sweet.

Sophie stared at Gizmo,
especially his shoes.
"Hattest du einen schlechten Morgen?
I mean, what happened to you?"

Gizmo told Sophie,
all about his being late.
And if he doesn't pass tomorrows exam,
he doesn't get to graduate.

He told her about the fairy tales,
and about the desk clerk who tricked him.
They both laughed about the pee pad moment,
and Gizmo's terrible first impression.

"It's true Germany is a Country,
built on rules and respect.
We won't keep you waiting,
so that's also what we expect."

"We may work hard,
but we play hard too.
Germany is known for festivals,
music, dancing, and chicken hats too."

They drove through wine country,
with its picture perfect scene.
With grapes planted on steep hill sides,
and rows and rows of green.

Some grapes are sour,
some grapes are sweet.
Some get stomped into wine,
and some are picked to eat.

"Germany is famous for Schnitzel, Bratwurst,
Sauerkraut, Pretzels, and Beer.
All celebrated at Oktoberfest,
attended by seven million people each year."

"Grab your Lederhosen,
or your Dirndl Kleid.
The chicken dance will play.
and you will dance all night."

The bus stopped in Nuremberg,
a city with a medieval castle and wall.
Now filled with happy people shopping,
but the city did once fall.

Fritz was telling the story,
about how Nuremburg was destroyed.
Where they stood was once rubble,
after six thousand bombs were deployed.

"The story could have ended,
and this would be just some old historic sight.
But someone had an idea,
to rebuild and make it right."

"One brick at a time,
determination unfurled.
Nuremberg is now known as the most famous,
Christmas Market in the World!"

"Christkind was born here,
he gives gifts to children.
Germans started decorating trees with apples,
starting the Christmas Tree tradition."

Nuremberg was beautiful,
and the gingerbread divine.
They took the fast train back to Cologne,
and made it in record time.

"Tomorrow is a big day,
make sure to get some rest.
Your final exam will be hands on.
This is your final test."

Gizmo stopped at the front desk,
to pick up the adapter he had to order.
He wasn't too thrilled with the clerk,
and his Grimm books of terror.

The desk clerk tried not to laugh,
when he saw Gizmo's shoes.
But he couldn't hold it back, he snorted,
"You're the one who snoozed!"

Gizmo was offended.
This was not cool!
What if he was late?
He would have flunked Service Dog School!

The clerk looked at Gizmo,
and stopped laughing.
"Gizmo you missed the whole lesson.
You do your own distracting."

"If it wasn't the books,
it would have been your phone.
Don't blame others,
for choices you made on your own."

"Your life is your story,
everyday a blank new page.
You get to chose the ending,
by what you do each day."

Gizmo thanked the desk clerk,
maybe he was right?
If he didn't stay up so late,
mornings wouldn't be such a fight.

Gizmo is the hero.
He's eating at the buffet.
Buzz Buzz Beep Biz...
He's up and ready for the day.

Sitting in the lobby,
he even beat Fritz.
He had on matching shoes,
and a miracle water spritz.

"The final exam is final.
You either pass or fail.
There is a damsel in distress,
inside of the Castle Bruhl."

"You have only seven minutes,
to assess the situation and find,
the lost lady and her medic alert,
and call the Krankenwagen in time."

Gizmo is the hero.
He really has a chance to be.
He feels sharp and confident,
ready to find the lost lady.

He ran down the staircase,
ears up like the big bad wolf.
The better to hear you with my dear.
He ran up towards the roof.

That's when he heard it,
it sounded just like his.
The alarm sound he dreaded each morning,
Buzz Buzz Beep Biz...

The lady was in the attic,
hiding behind a bin.
Gizmo called the ambulance.
It was a Graduation Win!

Fritz surprised the graduates,
with a trip along the Rhine,
to a Ritterfest,
that takes you back in time.

The festival looked like a fairy tale,
one with a happily ever after.
There were jousting knights in armor,
music, food, and laughter.

Fritz congratulated Gizmo,
"You have earned your Service Vest!
You learned that discipline,
is the highest form of self respect."

"Your life is your story.
It's yours to create.
You can settle for good,
or Dare to be Great!"

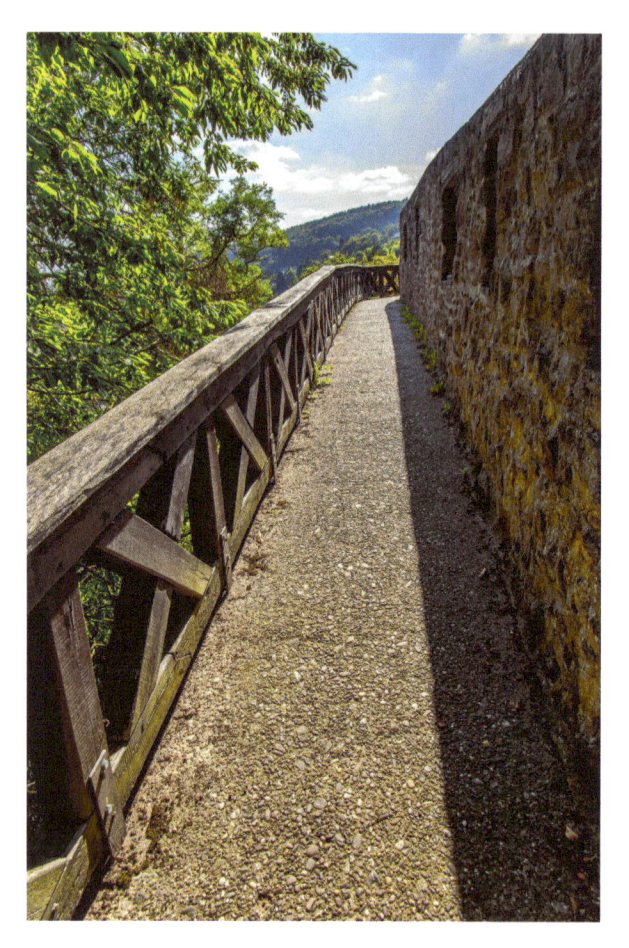

ABOUT THE AUTHOR

Heidi Heisel

Gizmo and I traveled to Germany in 2019. The Service Dog trainer's name, Fritz, was my dad's name. He passed away three years before I found Gizmo. I still miss his heavy accent. My sister and I were born in Germany, me in Dillingen/Saarland, and Monika in Phaffenhofen an der Ilm, Bayern.

ABOUT THE ILLUSTRATOR

River Wilson

River Wilson is Heidi's grandson. He is a Junior at the University of North Texas majoring in Marketing. He is a talented artist, fashion designer and world traveler.

GLOSSARY

Wilkommen in Deutschland – Welcome to Germany

Auf Wiedersehen – Goodbye

Du riechst gut! – You smell good.

Hattest du einen schlechten Morgan? – Did you have a bad morning?

Lederhosen –Leather shorts worn by German Men

Dirndl Kleid – Apron Dress worn by German Ladies

Ritterfest –A knights Festival

Krankenwagen – Ambulance

THE END

www.ingramcontent.com/pod-product compliance
Lightning Source LLC
Chambersburg PA
CBHW041417010526
44107CB00016B/1199